T0380298

OTHER MEDITATION BOOKS

BY

PHILIP KRILL

Listening to the Fathers - *A Year of Neo-patristic Reflections*

Le Point Vierge - *Meditations on the Mystery of Presence*

Praying with the Fathers - *A Year
of Neo-patristic Meditations*

Gelassenheit - *Day by Day with Meister Eckhart*

Mushin - *Meditations on the Mystery of Mindfulness*

Divine Kenosis - *Day-by-Day with Hans Urs von Balthasar*

Mawlānā

Contemplating

LOVE

with

Rumi

PHILIP KRILL

authorHOUSE®

AuthorHouse™
1663 Liberty Drive
Bloomington, IN 47403
www.authorhouse.com
Phone: 833-262-8899

© 2024 Philip Krill. All rights reserved.

No part of this book may be reproduced, stored in a retrieval system, or
transmitted by any means without the written permission of the author.

Published by AuthorHouse 04/03/2024

ISBN: 979-8-8230-2474-7 (sc)
ISBN: 979-8-8230-2475-4 (e)

Editorial Assistance: Jessi Livengood

Print information available on the last page.

Any people depicted in stock imagery provided by Getty Images are models,
and such images are being used for illustrative purposes only.
Certain stock imagery © Getty Images.

This book is printed on acid-free paper.

Because of the dynamic nature of the Internet, any web addresses or links contained in
this book may have changed since publication and may no longer be valid. The views
expressed in this work are solely those of the author and do not necessarily reflect the views
of the publisher, and the publisher hereby disclaims any responsibility for them.

To

Jessi Livengood

Well done, good and faithful servant!'

Matthew 25:23

Love is the bridge between you and everything.[1]

Rumi

[1] All quotations by Rumi in this book are sourced from: Rumi. AZQuotes.com, Wind and Fly LTD, 2024. https://www.azquotes.com/quote/501154.

Contents

Introduction

The phrase, 'Divine Love,' is tautological. 'God is love, and those who abide in love abide in God and God in them' (cf. 1 Jn. 4:8, 16).

Few have appreciated the ecstatic depths of the truth that 'God is love' more than Mawlānā Jalāl al-Dīn al-Rūmī. Like his spiritual mentor, Shams al-Dīn of Tabrīz, Rumi saw the whole of creation as a loving extension of, and participation in, the incomparable Source of Divine Love.

Following his life-changing encounter with Shams, Rumi spent the remainder of his days giving poetic expression to his experience of Divine Love. Much of Rumi's poetry was composed in a state of ecstasy, often induced by the music of the flute or the drum. Rumi also accompanied his verses by a whirling dance, and many of his poems were composed to be sung in Sufi musical gatherings.

These excerpts from the writings of Rumi are offered as easy access into the Mystery of Divine Love, especially for those who find religion tedious or tawdry. I pray that the reader will discover in the poetry of Rumi an immediate experience of Divine Love that religion often occludes.

Easter 2024

Love Divine

2

Let the beauty of what you love be what you do.

Meditation

Nothing done apart from love avails us anything. When who we are, what we love, and what we do elide, we become instruments and extensions of divine Love.

Prayer

Integrate us into Your divine Love, O God. Make our lives a seamless act of compassion.

3

In your light I learn how to love. In your beauty, how to make poems. You dance inside my chest where no one sees you, but sometimes I do, and that sight becomes this art.

Meditation

Internal vision inspires works of love. The light of divine Love transfigures those who give themselves to it.

Prayer

Divinize us with Your indwelling love, O God. Make us translucent with Your ineffable beauty.

4

Let yourself be drawn by the stronger pull of that which you truly love.

Meditation

Love has us, not us it. The pull of love will ultimately lead us to love's divine Source.

Prayer

Grant us the grace to go with the flow of love, O God. Immerse us in the Fountainhead of Your Love.

5

This is love: to fly toward a secret sky ... First, to let go of life [then,] finally, to take a step without feet.

Meditation

Love takes us out of ourselves into a magical space above and beyond the ordinary. Love takes us to heaven before we depart this world.

Prayer

Grant us a taste of eternity in all our human loves, O God. Reveal Yourself as the Source and Satisfaction of our loving desires.

6

Listen with ears of tolerance! See through the eyes of compassion! Speak with the language of love.

Meditation

Nothing done apart from love has lasting worth. One glance of pure love redeems a lifetime of dark looks.

Prayer

Dispel the darkness from our souls, O God. Illumine us with Your compassion that we might be instruments of Your divine Love.

7

Only from the heart can you touch the sky ... Reason is powerless in the expression of Love.

Meditation

Heaven is not beyond the clouds, it's just beyond our fears.[2] Thinking generates fear, doubt and insecurity; love gives birth to beauty, beatitude and bliss.

Prayer

Show us that the way to heaven passes through the heart, O God. Show us that the highway to heaven *is* heaven for those who love.

---

[2] A line from Garth Brook's song, *Belleau Wood*.

8

Love is the bridge between you and everything.

Meditation

Love is the divine *Pontifex.*[3] Like Jacob's Ladder, love allows us to traverse from earth to heaven and back again.

Prayer

Show us that the bridge we seek to build with others has already been built by You, O God. Show us that love makes heavenly connection possible.

---

[3] Literally, 'Bridge builder.'

9

Believe in love's infinite journey, for it is your own, for you are love. Love is life.

Meditation

Love is not something we do, it's something we are. 'God is love' (cf. 1 Jn. 4:8) and we are finite extensions of God's divine Love.

Prayer

Awaken us to our identity as icons of Your divine Love, O God. Show us that in loving others, You divinize the world.

10

Both light and shadow are the dance of love ... Every moment is made glorious by the light of love.

Meditation

Love reveals 'good vs. evil' as an expression of evil. Love is beyond all distinctions, makes no distinctions, and divinizes those who refuse to judge.

Prayer

Awaken us to the deceptions of dialectical judgment, O God. Show us that 'Love bears all things, believes all things, hopes all things, endures all things' (cf. 1 Cor. 13:7).

11

Out beyond ideas of wrongdoing and right-doing there is a field. I'll meet you there.

Meditation

Like a rocket ship headed into space, we experience a blissful peace once we break through the gravitational pull of our earthly thoughts. Leaving behind our deluded judgments, we break through into the pure space of God's infinite goodness.

Prayer

Draw us up and out of our earth-bound ways of thinking, O God. Pull us into the glorious spaciousness of Your unbounded Love.

Religion of Love

13

Religion seeks grace and favor, but those who gamble these away are God's favorites, for they neither put God to the test nor knock at the door of gain and loss.

Meditation

Those who ask nothing of God receive everything from God. Religion fulfills itself in every act of loving relinquishment.

Prayer

Free us from self-interest, O God. Teach us to love You and others for Your own sakes, neither counting the cost nor seeking a reward.

14

Be certain that in the religion of love there are no believers and unbelievers. Love embraces all.

Meditation

Love is 'catholic,' i.e., universal and indiscriminate. Nothing and no one can escape the divinizing power of love.

Prayer

Take us beyond the world of belief and unbelief, O God. Show us the transcendent power of love.

15

You think you are alive because you breathe air? Shame on you, that you are alive in such a limited way. Die in Love and stay alive forever.

Meditation

Love is stronger than death (cf. Song of Songs 8:6). Dying to self-interest for the sake of love, we taste eternal life.

Prayer

Breathe in us the air of divine Love, O God. Fill us with the Love that raises the dead to life.

16

God turns you from one feeling to another and teaches by means of opposites so that you will have two wings to fly, not one.

Meditation

Both consolation and desolation can turn us towards God, towards Love. All things work together in the lives of those who know God (cf. Rom. 8:28).

Prayer

In Your Love, opposites are reconciled, O God. Use the antinomies of this world to transport us into Your divine Embrace.

17

Explanation by the tongue makes most things clear, but love unexplained is clearer.

Meditation

'The heart has reasons the head knows not of.'[4] The *logos* (logic) of love defies explanation.

Prayer

Help us abide in Your why-less Love, O God.[5] Reveal the divine Love whose divinizing power needs no explanation.

---

[4] Blaise Paschal, *Pensées,* 277.
[5] God's 'why-less love' is a phrase common in the writings of Meister Eckhart. See: *An Introduction to the Medieval Mystics of Europe,* Paul E. Szarmach, ed. Albany, State University of New York Press, 1984, 253.

18

I merged so completely with love, and was so fused, that I became love and love became me.

Meditation

'God became man so man could become God.'[6] The aim of every religion is intimate union with the Loving Source of our existence (God).

Prayer

Elevate us to divine union with You, O God. Assimilate us without dissolution into the Mystery of Your eternal Love.

---

[6] A common theme of the early church fathers, e.g., St. Athanasius, *On the Incarnation*, 54.

19

It is certain that an atom of goodness on the path of faith is never lost.

Meditation

Every act of faith is a moment of openness to divine Love. God is the Source and Satisfaction of such faith.

Prayer

Open us to the infinity of Your Love, O God. Show us that our very desire to know You is Your Presence within us.

20

I have been a seeker and I still am, but I stopped asking the books and the stars. I started listening to the teaching of my soul.

Meditation

Seek God from within, not from without. Only in the heart can God be intuitively known and loved.

Prayer

Turn our attention inward so we can hear the whispers of Your Spirit, O God. Satisfy our seeking in the depths of our souls.

21

The lovers of God have no religion but God alone.

Meditation

Religion fulfills itself in love. 'Those who abide in love abide in God' (cf. 1 Jn. 4:16).

Prayer

Form us in the religion that takes us beyond religion, O God. Show us that You dwell not in dogma but in the unapproachable Light of divine Love.

22

Love gambles away every gift God bestows. Without cause God gave us being, without cause give it back again. Gambling yourself away is beyond any religion.

Meditation

True faith abandons everything for the sake of Love, including religion. The purpose of religion is to move us beyond itself into the Mystery of divine Love.

Prayer

Free our spirits from every restriction that passes as religion, O God. Show us that a truly religious heart gambles away everything to win the pearl of great price (cf. Mt. 13:46).

God of Love

24

What I want also wants me, is looking for me and attracting me. What you are seeking is also seeking you. There is a great secret here for anyone who can grasp it.

Meditation

God is closer to us than we are to ourselves.[7] Apprehending the immediacy of God, we enter God's kingdom.

Prayer

Show us that our search for You is of a piece with Your quest for us, O God. Grant us to experience You in the depths of our hearts.

---

[7] As St. Augustine says, God is *"Interior intimo meo et superior summo meo"* ('higher than my highest and more inward than my innermost self') (*Confessions* III, 6, 11).

25

A candle never loses any of its light while lighting up another candle.

Meditation

God is a Mystery of super-abundance. God bestows 'grace upon grace,' blessing upon blessing (cf. Jn. 1:16).

Prayer

Banish our zero-sum approach to Your divine Love, O God. Show us that You *cannot not* give Yourself to those who come to You poor in spirit but rich with holy desire.

26

The inspiration you seek is already within you. Be silent and listen.

Meditation

That which draws us is that which we seek. God is the Source, Summit and Satisfaction of our desire for God.

Prayer

Show us our powerlessness without You, O God. Show us that 'apart from You we can do nothing,' but in You we 'can do all things' (cf. Jn. 15:5; Php. 4:13).

27

I looked for God. I went to a temple and I didn't find him there. I went to a church and I didn't find him there. I went to a mosque and I didn't find him there. Then finally I looked in my heart and there he was.

Meditation

We can no sooner find God outside ourselves than our eyes can see themselves. God is everywhere and nowhere, seen only with the eyes of the heart.

Prayer

Teach us to rest in learned ignorance, O God. End our quest to discover You anywhere but in the infinite depths of love.

28

Love cannot be described. It must be tasted.

Meditation

We thirst for knowledge, hunger for love, and yearn for beauty. Our desires for love, truth and beauty are insatiable.

Prayer

Satisfy our spiritual longings, O God. Let us forever savor the sweetness of Your divine Love.

29

If in thirst you drink water from a cup, you see God in it. Those who are not in love with God will see only their own faces in it.

Meditation

For those who love God, even a cup of cold water is a sacrament of God's Presence. For all others, it is simply hydration.

Prayer

Slake our thirst with the living-water of Your Love, O God (cf. Jn. 7:38). Root us near Your River of Life so we may bear abundant fruit in every season (cf. Rev. 22:2).

30

Remember God so much that you are forgotten. Let the caller and the called disappear; be lost in the call.

Meditation

Remembrance of God is forgetfulness of self. In the space of self-forgetfulness, we hear the Lord calling our name.

Prayer

'If today we hear Your voice, harden not our hearts,' O God (cf. Heb. 3:15). Turn our attention from ourselves so we can hear the whispers of Your Spirit.

31

'Lo, I am with you always' means when you look for God, God is in the look of your eyes, in the thought of looking, nearer to you than your self, or things that have happened to you. There's no need to go outside.

Meditation

'Enlightenment' means becoming increasingly aware of the immediacy of God's Presence. The desire for God is the Presence of God, just as God is present as the Source and Satisfaction of every human desire.

Prayer

Awaken us to Your Presence in all of our heart's desires, O God. Show us that in desiring anything, we are desiring You.

32

Whenever you are alone, remind yourself that God has sent everyone else away so that there is only you and Him.

Meditation

God desires intimate union with all those he has created. Let it be to us as God desires (cf. Lk. 1:38).

Prayer

Consummate Your call to intimacy with us, O God. Bring to ecstatic completion the union of love You desire with us.

33

I said: what about my pain and sorrow? God said: Stay with it. The wound is the place where the light enters you.

Meditation

Breakdown precedes breakthrough. Complete collapse is the precondition for spiritual awakening.

Prayer

Teach us to 'suffer' - i.e., 'allow' - our pain to speak to us, O God. Show us that when 'suffering' our pain, the light of Your Love dawns upon us.

Letting Go in Love

35

Trust means you're ready to risk what you currently have.

Meditation

Perfect trust dispels all fear (cf. 1 Jn. 4:8). Risk is the path to redemption.

Prayer

Increase our trust in You, O God. Show us that letting go of fear, doubt and insecurity is the road to serenity.

36

Put your thoughts to sleep, do not let them cast a shadow over the moon of your heart.

Meditation

Purity of heart requires emptiness of thought. Silence is the ambient sound in the inner chamber of the soul.

Prayer

Illumine our hearts with Your divine Wisdom, O God. Keep our thinking from obscuring Your crystal-clear Presence.

37

Let go of thinking. Let go of your mind and then be mindful. Close your ears and listen!

Meditation

Mindfulness is attentiveness unobscured by thought. God manifests his Presence in the space of No-Mind (*Mushin*).[8]

Prayer

Help us relinquish our thoughts so we can intuit Your Presence, O God. Divinize us in the silence of mindfulness.

---

[8] See Philip Krill, *Mushin: Meditations on Mindfulness.*

38

You have been stony for too many years. Try something different. Surrender.

Meditation

Letting go (*Gelassenheit*)[9] is the essence of love. Intimacy is a function of granting the beloved the freedom to be oneself.

Prayer

Keep us out of the POOP (Power over other People), O God. Show us that letting go is the measure of true love.

---

[9] See Philip Krill, *Gelassenheit: Day-by-Day with Meister Eckhart*.

39

From deep inside my soul cries out: Do not wait, surrender for the sake of love.

Meditation

Spiritual victory is won through interior surrender. Relinquishing our illusions of control, we receive blessings in abundance.

Prayer

Inspire us to surrender to the power of the present moment, O God. Grant us the joy of living in Your eternal Now.

40

The intellect and the senses investigate cause and effect. The spiritual seeker surrenders to the wonder.

Meditation

Awe is the natural response to the miracle of existence. Awareness of the goodness of being is bliss *(Sacchidānanda)*.[10]

Prayer

Grant us the blissful intuition of being, O God. Fill our hearts with joy at the wonder of existence.

---

[10] *Sacchidānanda is* a Hindu term that connotes the divine Bliss *(Ananda)* that arises within us when our Awareness *(Chit)* rests in Being *(Sat)*, not in thinking.

41

Stop, open up, surrender the beloved blind silence. Stay there until you see you're looking at the light with infinite eyes.

Meditation

It takes a while for our spiritual vision to adjust to the uncreated Light and Love of God. Purgation is required to enter Paradise.

Prayer

Grant us patience in attaining Your kingdom, O God. Teach us to abide in anticipatory silence until You come at the hour we least expect (cf. Mt. 24:44).

42

I am dying into your mystery, and dying, I am now no other than that mystery. I open to your majesty as an orchard welcomes rain, and twenty times that.

Meditation

The Love of God is a gentle rain and warming sun that gives life to a dying world (cf. Mt. 5:45). Opening to the Mystery of God, we blossom with unanticipated fruitfulness.

Prayer

Irrigate our parched and arid souls, O God. Bring to fruition the seeds of divine life You have implanted within us.

43

Like the sun, only when you set in the west can you rise in the east.

Meditation

Dying, we rise to ever-new life; letting go, we are lifted into divine glory.

Prayer

Show us that surrender is the way to salvation, O God. Show us that complete relinquishment is the *sine quo non* for resurrection.

44

*To become spiritual, you must die to self, and come alive in the Lord.
Only then will the mysteries of God fall from your lips.*

Meditation

We must have the heart of God to speak the words of God.
This requires the complete evacuation of self-interest.

Prayer

Divest us of self-interest so we can witness to Your divine
Wisdom, O God. Purify our hearts so our lips can better
proclaim Your praise (cf. Ps. 51:15)

Suffering in Love

46

Only when you suffer the pangs and tribulations of exile will you truly enjoy your homecoming.

Meditation

Absence makes the heart grow fonder. Separation slows us down long enough to discover our true priorities.

Prayer

Show us that estrangement is the path to enlightenment, O God. Turn our experience of exile into the ecstasy of trusting You.

47

The sweetness and delights of the resting-place are in proportion to the pain endured on the Journey.

Meditation

No pain, no gain. All the way to heaven - including our stumbles and falls - *is* heaven.

Prayer

Shine upon us as the Light at the end of life's tunnel, O God. Show us that our struggles on the journey enhance the bliss of our arrival.

48

Longing is the core of mystery. longing itself brings the cure.

Meditation

Holiness consists exclusively in holy desire. Indifference to the fruits of our actions[11] is the perfection pleasing to God.

Prayer

Fill us with divine longing, O God. Show us that our desire to please You is most pleasing to You.

---

[11] Known as *Karma Yoga,* acting with indifference to the fruits of our actions is expressed clearly in the *Bhagavad Gita* (2.47): '*You have a right to perform your prescribed duties, but you are not entitled to the fruits of your actions. Never consider yourself to be the cause of the results of your activities, nor be attached to inaction.'*

49

There's no cure except the retreat into love for the suffering of subtly afflicted hearts.

Meditation

Compassion comforts the hurting hearts of others. Empathy is an extension of God's healing Presence.

Prayer

Allow our compassion to compensate for what our words of comfort fail to achieve, O God. Use our empathy to convey Your healing love.

50

O Seeker, pain and suffering make one aware of God.

Meditation

God permits suffering to encourage surrender. When the pain of holding on becomes greater than the pain of letting go, we let go.

Prayer

Help us recognize Your divine summons in our suffering, O God. Use our pain to spur the interior surrender that brings us Your peace.

51

Why are you knocking at every other door? Go, knock at the door of your own heart.

Meditation

God dwells in us, and we have our being in God (cf. Acts 17:28). Knowing ourselves one with God is the condition for loving others as God loves us (cf. Jn. 15:9-12).

Prayer

We look for love in all the wrong places, O God. Summon us to abide with You so we can love others as You love us.

52

The ground submits to the sky and suffers whatever comes. Tell me, is the earth worse for giving in like that?

Meditation

As the earth opens itself to the rain and shine from the heavens, so can we open ourselves to the Infinite. When we do so, God deifies us with his life-giving Spirit and uncreated Light.

Prayer

Inspire us to seek Your heavenly illumination, O God. Help us turn our faces towards You, just as the earth opens itself to the sky.

53

Don't get lost in your pain, know that one day your pain will become your cure.

Meditation

Pain punctures our pretensions and opens us to the comforting peace of God. Letting go of control, we fall into God's Embrace.

Prayer

Teach us to accept 'the thorns in our flesh' that keep us humble, O God (cf. 2 Cor. 3:8). When we are brought low in our pain, lift us up in Your divine mercy.

54

When I run after what I think I want, my days are a furnace of stress and anxiety; if I sit in my own place of patience, what I need flows to me, and without pain.

Meditation

If something doesn't fit, don't force it. Flow, not force, is the generative power of love.

Prayer

Cause Your Love to flow through us, O God. Make us channels of Your life-giving Spirit.

55

Sorrow prepares you for joy. It violently sweeps everything out of your house, so that new joy can find space to enter ... Whatever sorrow shakes from your heart, far better things will take their place.

Meditation

Sorrow is the purifying water of the Spirit. Tears of sorrow cleanse the soul so tears of joy can take their place.

Prayer

Reveal sorrow as the flip-side of joy, O God. Show us that our grief is an inverted reflection of the infinite Love that our hearts desire.

Heart of Love

57

Goodbyes are only for those who love with their eyes. For those who love with heart and soul there is no such thing as separation.

Meditation

Absence makes the heart grow fonder. In the spaciousness of our hearts, intimacy becomes possible.

Prayer

Life can be a series of painful partings, O God. Show us that absence makes our hearts grow fonder when we abide in Your Eternal Now.

58

I found the Divine within my Heart.

Meditation

God is best discovered interiorly, as God is closer to us than we are to ourselves.[12]

Prayer

Awaken us to Your indwelling Presence, O God. Help us discover You as the Source of our desire to know You.

---

[12] See above, n. 7.

59

You have to keep breaking your heart until it opens.

Meditation

God heals the brokenhearted (cf. Ps. 147:3). A humble, contrite heart God will not spurn (cf. Ps. 51:17).

Prayer

Open us to Your divine salve, O God. Show Yourself as the Divine Physician who is pleased to heal our wounds.

60

Your heart is the size of an ocean. Go find yourself in its hidden depths.

Meditation

Entering the infinite depths of our hearts, we find ourselves immersed in an ocean of Divine Mercy. Here our lives are 'hidden with Christ in God' (cf. Col. 3:3).

Prayer

Remind us that Your kingdom is within us, O God (cf. Lk. 10:9; 17:21). Awaken us to Your indwelling Presence.

61

Find the sweetness in your own heart, then you may find the sweetness in every heart.

Meditation

Charity begins at home. Love of neighbor presumes an appreciation of the unique person God has made each of us to be.

Prayer

Lead us into the sweet-spot of our existence, O God. Awaken us to Your Presence in the *le point vierge* of our being.[13]

---

[13] *Le Point Vierge* (French) means 'virginal point.' Made famous by Thomas Merton's use of this term in his book, *Conjectures of a Guilty Bystander,* Merton borrowed this phrase from the writings of Sufism scholar, Louis Massingnon. See also: Philip Krill, *Le Point Vierge: Meditations on the Mystery of Presence.*

62

There is a window from one heart to another heart.

Meditation

Openness makes intimacy possible. Without openness, togetherness remains an illusion.

Prayer

Unite us in our common experience of pure awareness, O God. Open the windows of our souls so Your life-giving Spirit can blow through us.[14]

---

[14] As the poet, Hafiz says, *'I am a hole in a flute that the Christ's breath moves through ... listen to this music.'*

63

The only lasting beauty is the beauty of the heart.

Meditation

As external beauty fades, internal beauty grows ever more apparent. Our bodies are instruments of our spirits, our eyes the windows of our souls.

Prayer

Make us living sacraments of Your divine Love, O God. Transfigure us with Your uncreated Light.

64

That which is false troubles the heart, but truth brings joyous tranquility.

Meditation

Consolation is the way of truth. Discordant notes of falsehood create a disturbance in the Force of God's cosmic Love.

Prayer

Fill us with the joy of Your universal Love, O God. Show us that, in You, love and truth are one.

65

Everyone has been made for some particular work, and the desire for that work has been put in every heart.

Meditation

Our personal missions are as unique as our fingerprints. Knowing who we are and what we are created to do are inseparable.

Prayer

Show us the joy of staying in our own lane, O God. Help us focus on our unique callings to the exclusion of comparisons with, and judgements of, others.

66

Only from the heart can you touch the sky.

Meditation

Heaven is accessed through the heart. In the deepest center of our being (*le point vierge*) the Light from on high dawns upon us.

Prayer

Illumine us from within, O God. Let the radiance of Your heavenly love transform us from the inside out.

In the Eye of Love

68

Look at love with the eyes of your heart.

Meditation

The gaze of love penetrates appearances. True beauty appears in the mirror of our souls.

Prayer

Teach us to see with the eyes of the heart, O God. Sharpen our interior vision so we can discern the deep-down beauty of every person we meet.

69

Put yourself behind my eyes and see me as I see myself, for I have chosen to dwell in a place you cannot see.

Meditation

Just as our eyes cannot see themselves, so God cannot be known by our minds. When we pause from our analysis, God can be tacitly apprehended.

Prayer

Draw us into the luminous darkness where You indwell us, O God. Show us that Your infinite Love occupies the interior space of letting go.

70

Everything that is made beautiful and fair and lovely is made for the eye of one who sees.

Meditation

Reality gives itself to the soul fully open to the graciousness of being. The cosmos itself appears perfectly pristine to the virginal heart.

Prayer

Like attracts like. The goodness and beauty of creation gives itself without reservation to the gracious and beautiful heart.

71

Listen with ears of tolerance! See through the eyes of compassion! Speak with the language of love.

Meditation

'Judge not, lest you be judged' (cf. Mt. 7:1). One moment of complete compassion redeems a lifetime of criticism and complaint.

Prayer

Jettison our fears, doubts and insecurities, O God. Fill us instead with Your divine compassion.

72

The light which shines in the eye is really the light of the heart ... The light which fills the heart is the light of God, which is pure and separate from the light of intellect and sense.

Meditation

The 'I' with which we see God is the 'I' with which God sees us.[15] Our consciousness is a participation in God's self-knowledge.

Prayer

In Your Light we see light, O God (cf. Ps. 36:9). Illumine us from within with Your uncreated Light.

---

[15] Saying attributed, without reference, to Meister Eckhart. See: https://www.goodreads.com/quotes/7169-the-eye-through-which-i-see-god-is-the-same.

73

Close both eyes to see with the other eye.

Meditation

Our 'third eye' is the eye of the heart. It is God's answer to the evil eye.

Prayer

Close our eyes to evil and enlighten us with Your Wisdom, O God. Send Your Holy *Sophia* to illumine us from within.

74

Open your eyes, for this world is only a dream.

Meditation

Awakening to divine Love is like awaking from a bad dream.
The relief is indescribable.

Prayer

Draw us into the ecstatic awareness of Your all-consuming
Love, O God. Banish our nightmares with Your vision of
Peace.

75

Look at me not with an outward eye but with inward vision of the heart;
follow me there and see how unencumbered we become.

Meditation

In a heart filled with divine Love, debates and divisions
dissolve. God creates 'holy communion' with those who
connect heart-to-heart.

Prayer

Cor ad cor loquitur.[16] Teach us to harken to the voice of the
heart, O God. Open our ears to the whispers of Your Spirit.

---

[16] 'Heart speaks to heart': The motto of St. John Henry Newman.

76

Never lose hope, my heart, miracles dwell in the invisible. If the whole world turns against you, keep your eyes on the Friend.

Meditation

'It is only in the heart that one can see rightly; what is essential is invisible to the eye.'[17]

Prayer

Illumine our inner vision, O God. Show us Your face in the depths of our hearts.

---

[17] Antoine de Saint Exupéry, *The Little Prince.*

77

I am bewildered by the magnificence of your beauty, and wish to see you with a hundred eyes . . . I am in the house of mercy, and my heart is a place of prayer.

Meditation

Love is blind to the faults of the beloved. Perfect love overlooks the faults of the enemy (cf. Lk. 6:27).

Prayer

Divinize our love, O God. Make us perfect as You are perfect (cf. Mt. 5:48).

Joy of Love

79

When you feel a peaceful joy, that's when you are near truth.

Meditation

Relief arises when truth is revealed. The deeper the truth, the greater our joy.

Prayer

Show us there is nothing to fear, but everything to gain, in discovering the truth, O God. Show us that knowing the truth will set us free (cf. Jn. 8:32).

80

When you do things from your soul, you feel a river moving in you, a joy.

Meditation

The living water of God's Spirit arises unbidden from the wellspring of our being. In the virginal point (*le point vierge*) of our souls, God speaks in silence.

Prayer

Attune us to the silent music of Your Spirit, O God. Fill us with Your inexplicable joy.

81

Make peace with the universe. Take joy in it. It will turn to gold.
Resurrection will be now. Every moment, a new beauty.

Meditation

All is pure to the pure. Approach the world with a virginal
heart and every creature will be your beloved.

Prayer

Grant us eyes of mercy, O God. Purify our vision so we can
behold the world bathed in Your supernal beauty.

82

If you love someone, you are always joined with them - in joy, in absence, in solitude, in strife.

Meditation

Communion overcomes every separation. Absence enhances intimacy for those who abide in love.

Prayer

Show us that nothing can separate us from Your Love, O God (cf. Rom. 8:38). Establish us in communion with You so we can love others as You love us.

83

Everything you see has its roots in the unseen world. The source they come from is eternal, growing, branching out, giving new life and new joy.

Meditation

God is ever-greater, ever-more. Abiding in the Mystery of God, every moment is a fresh revelation of divine Love.

Prayer

Open us to the eternal freshness of Your self-disclosure, O God. Awaken us to the always-surprising joy of knowing You.

84

The hurt you embrace becomes joy.

Meditation

Acceptance brings peace. Total acceptance (without resentment) brings perfect peace.

Prayer

Grant us a share in Your non-resistant Love, O God. Inspire our heartfelt *Fiat* (consent) to all that happens in life.

85

Joy lives concealed in grief.

Meditation

Grief is the underbelly of love, and joy is the leading symptom of love.

Prayer

Grant us joy in the midst of grief, O God. Reveal the pain of our losses as a sharing in Your long-suffering Love.

86

Patience is the key to joy.

Meditation

'Letting be' solves most of our problems. Patience affords us the prudence that makes responsible action possible.

Prayer

Grant us a share in Your divine Mercy, O God. Make us as patient with others as You are with us.

87

I sail with you on the ocean of my dreams ... where we give praises for our joy and happiness, where our love intertwines with Love for all things.

Meditation

Love is a seamless garment. When we love another, all things become lovely.

Prayer

Clothe us in Your divine Love, O God. Fill us with such grace that all things appear beautiful.

88

The soul is here for its own joy.

Meditation

We are created to share in the joy of the Lord (cf. Jn. 15:11). Ecstasy is our origin and our destiny.[18]

Prayer

Fill us with the joy of Your creative Love, O God. Divinize us with Your uncreated Light.

---

[18] See Alvin Kimmel, *Destined for Joy: The Gospel of Universal Salvation.*

Harmonics of Love

90

All your anxiety is because of your desire for harmony. Seek disharmony, then you will gain peace.

Meditation

Attempts to control the rough-edges of reality cause frustration. Accepting reality on its own terms brings peace.

Prayer

Show us that acceptance is the answer to all our problems today, O God. Teach us to embrace chaos as the path to peace.

91

The life of this world is nothing but the harmony of opposites.

Meditation

Push and pull, woof and warp, yin and yang: what God has united, human beings must not divide.

Prayer

Save us from turning polarities into polemics, O God. Teach us to love difference without division, otherness without alienation.

92

Lamps are different, but light is the same.

Meditation

The prism of creation reflects God's uncreated Light in an infinite number of ways. In God's Light, we see light (cf. Ps. 36:9).

Prayer

Help us see created beauty as a reflection of Your uncreated Light, O God. Keep us from mistaking the lamps for the Light.

93

Both light and shadow are the dance of Love. Every moment is made glorious by the light of Love.

Meditation

Even the darkness is not dark to those abiding in God (cf. Ps. 139:12). The Light of God casts no shadow, revealing even the darkness as a reflection of love.

Prayer

Bathe us in Your shadowless Love, O God. Illumine our every moment, even the dark ones, with Your uncreated Light.

94

Like a sculptor, carve a friend out of stone. Realize that your inner sight is blind and try to see a treasure in everyone.

Meditation

Where others saw only a block of marble, Michelangelo saw the Pietà. A vision of divine Love reveals every person as a masterpiece of God.

Prayer

Grant us an inner vision that bathes Your world in beauty, O God. Help us recognize Your image and likeness in every person we encounter.

95

In things spiritual, there is no partition, no number, no individuals. How sweet is the oneness - unearth the treasure of unity!

Meditation

All things that arise must converge.[19] The cosmos is a seamless garment, sustained in existence through union with its Source.

Prayer

Open our eyes to the fundamental union of all things, O God. Keep us from dividing what You have united.

---

[19] Borrowed from the title of a collection of short stories by Flannery O'Connor.

96

In real existence there is only unity.

Meditation

We see divisions where God sees only communion. All that exists holds together in God's creative Love (cf. Col. 1:17).

Prayer

Awaken us to the unity of all things, O God. Grant us the peace that comes from knowing that nothing real can be threatened and nothing unreal exists.[20]

---

[20] The opening lines and summary statement of *A Course on Miracles*.

The water in the stream may have changed many times, but the reflection of the moon and the stars remains the same.

Meditation

God's Presence is unaffected by the constant change in creation. 'There lives the dearest freshness deep down things' that never fades.[21]

Prayer

Help us discern Your divine grandeur in everything we behold, O God. Help us behold the beauty of the universe 'in a single grain of sand.'[22]

---

[21] A line from Gerard Manley Hopkins' poem, *God's Grandeur.*
[22] An image drawn from William Blake's poem, *Auguries of Innocence.*

98

Love is the energizing elixir of the universe, the cause and effect of all harmony.

Meditation

Love is symphonic[23] - it unites all things in differentiated union.

Prayer

Draw us into the harmonics of divine Love, O God. Attune our hearts to the music of the spheres.

---

[23] Borrowed from the title of a book by Hans Urs von Balthasar.

99

Love has no cause, it is the astrolabe of God's secrets ... Every moment is made glorious by the light of Love.

Meditation

God's Love is a why-less Love.[24] Existence itself is unexplainable apart from God's creative act of Love.

Prayer

Arrest us with Your unconditioned Love, O God. Show us that Your unprompted benevolence is the Fountainhead of the world's beauty.

---

[24] See above, n. 5.

Fearless Love

101

When you see the sun setting, wait for the rising. Why worry about a sunset or a fading moon?

Meditation

Every Now is a new opportunity. Worry and regret gain no purchase in the present moment.

Prayer

Dispel the darkness of worry with the light of Your eternal Now, O God. Deliver us of depression with the promise of the present.

102

Forget safety. Live where you fear to live. Destroy your reputation. Be notorious.

Meditation

Be bold, be brief, be gone - good advice for preachers and prophets alike.

Prayer

Grant us a share in Your prodigal love, O God. Teach us to throw caution to the wind when following the inspirations of Your Spirit.

103

Start a huge, foolish project, like Noah ... it makes absolutely no difference what people think of you.

Meditation

The wisdom of the world is foolishness to God (cf. 1 Cor. 3:19). Become a holy fool, for God's sake.

Prayer

Prevent us from preening and posturing, O God. Dissolve our pretensions so we can live with the holy *parrhesia*[25] of Your saints.

---

[25] *Parrhesia* means 'to speak boldly,' including the obligation to speak the truth for the common good, even at personal risk.

104

I died as a mineral and became a plant, I died as a plant and rose to animal, I died as an animal and I was Man. Why should I fear? When was I less by dying?

Meditation

Death and resurrection are the watermark of creation. Death destroys nothing but changes everything.

Prayer

Reveal death as the opening to new and greater life, O God. Transform our vision of death into an opportunity for deeper trust.

105

Move, but don't move the way fear makes you move.

Meditation

Nothing born of fear bears fruit. Perfect love, however, drives out all fear (cf. 1 Jn. 4:8).

Prayer

Fill us with Your fearless love, O God. Replace our fears with the faith that can move mountains (cf. Mt. 17:20).

106

Move outside the tangle of fear-thinking. Live in silence.

Meditation

Thinking cannot solve the problems thinking creates. Inner silence is the antidote to the cacophony of fearful thoughts.

Prayer

Deliver us from fear-driven thinking, O God. Summons us into sacred silence.

107

Love is a river. Drink from it.

Meditation

If we do what we love and love what we do, we'll never work a day in our lives. Life is beautiful for those whose vacation is their vocation.

Prayer

Show us that all the way to heaven *is* heaven for those who know themselves loved by You, O God. Help us live the beauty we love.

108

The water said to the dirty one, 'Come here.' The dirty one said, 'I am too ashamed.' The water replied, 'How will your shame be washed away without me?

Meditation

God's desire to forgive is greater than our need for forgiveness. Only pride and shame prevent us from accepting God's infinite mercy.

Prayer

Wash us clean with the living water of Your Spirit, O God. Cleanse us of our guilt, shame and remorse with Your life-giving mercy.

109

Sell your cleverness and buy.

Meditation

Cleverness pays small dividends. Better to risk it all than to settle for diminishing returns.

Prayer

Expand our spiritual prodigality, O God. Help us invest all we have to buy Your pearls of great price (cf. Mt. 13:46).

110

Birds make great sky-circles of their freedom. How do they learn it? They fall and, by falling, they're given wings.

Meditation

Let go and let God. Plummeting into the depths of our hearts, we are catapulted into God's embrace.

Prayer

Show us that relinquishment and resurrection are a seamless mystery, O God. Grant us the grace of letting go so we can be lifted up into Your lap.

Printed in the United States
by Baker & Taylor Publisher Services